MARK YAMPOLSKY
VIOLONCELLO
TECHNIQUE
Edited by GORDON EPPERSON

ISBN 978-1-4234-0694-5

HAL•LEONARD®
CORPORATION
7777 W. BLUEMOUND RD. P.O. BOX 13819 MILWAUKEE, WI 53213

Visit Hal Leonard Online at
www.halleonard.com

Preface

The opportunity of offering this important work in violoncello pedagogy to an English-speaking public is yet another illustration of how much we have to gain from "cultural exchange." I do not know of another manual in the technical literature of cellists that so admirably combines brevity and comprehensiveness. Beyond this, however, Yampolsky accomplishes the still more difficult task of making the "dry bones" of our calling—scales and arpeggios—musically attractive in the settings he has provided for them.

What could easily have been a mechanical repitition of patterns from key to key has become, under the author's imaginative treatment, a richly-varied diet of rhythms and bowings. And where many manuals rely upon the teacher's ingenuity to multiply examples—a highly calculated risk—Yampolsky himself gives the variants in generous supply.

The author's introduction to the work states his aims lucidly. He is not rigid in prescribing the use to which the material of his book is to be put and he suggests that some teachers may wish to present the scales in a different "order." Well and good. I can foresee that others may wish to modify fingerings, particularly those who make greater use of "extensions" than Yampolsky; again, such changes are easily incorporated and will in no way lessen the value or wide usefulness of the book.

I therefore send it on as it came from his hands, confident that my enthusiasm for Yampolsky's admirable book will be shared by an increasing number of cellists who will find it an indispensable technical aid.

Gordon Epperson

Introduction

The study of scales and arpeggios in all their various bowed, fingered and rhythmic combinations is one of the major factors in the development of the technique of the right and left hands. The present volume aims to lighten the load and save time for the teacher by giving the student convenient material for daily work in these areas.

The collection includes scales; broken thirds; arpeggios of the tonic, subdominant, dominant seventh and diminished seventh chords, as well as augmented triads and "short" arpeggios; double stops in thirds, sixths, octaves, and tenths; triads and scales in chords.

Because various bowing, rhythmic, and finger combinations have been included, this book can to some extent replace etudes.

The keys are arranged in order of increasing complexity of signature: C Major and A Minor are followed by the keys with one accidental (G Major, E Minor, F Major, D Minor), leading to those with two sharps or flats (D Major, B Minor, B-flat Major, G Minor) and so on. This order, however, should by no means be thought of as obligatory and can be rearranged at the teacher's discretion. It is quite expedient, for example, during the study of a concerto or concert piece to practice the corresponding scale with its related material as given in this book and, at the same time, to incorporate the bowings and rhythms of the piece. Further, after studying each key at first in the simplest and most elementary bowings (as shown in C Major), it is beneficial to work out in each key the bowings and rhythms presented in this book with all the other keys.

The material presented here can be used, under the teacher's direction, not only in its fullest compass (four octaves), but also within the limits of three or even two octaves at earlier stages of the student's development. Harmonic minor scales have been omitted in order to keep the book to a reasonable size; but the student should play them, nevertheless, using (with rare exceptions) the fingerings of the melodic minor. It is important to note that the fingerings for double-stopped arpeggios are identical in the major and in the minor.

The accents in this volume are not intended to indicate a louder tone, but rather to aid in the attainment of rhythmic accuracy by means of a slight stress.

When a choice of fingerings is given, the scales should be practiced with both; but one should go on to the second fingering only after the first has been mastered.

Mark Yampolsky

Abbreviations

W . . . Whole Bow
L . . . Lower Half
U . . . Upper Half
M . . . Middle
Pt. . . Point
Fr. . . Frog

I . . . . A String
II . . . D String
III . . . G String
IV . . . C String

C MAJOR

Bowing variants for No. 1

Broken thirds

Arpeggios

a Tonic

b Sub-dominant

Dominant seventh

6

Variant

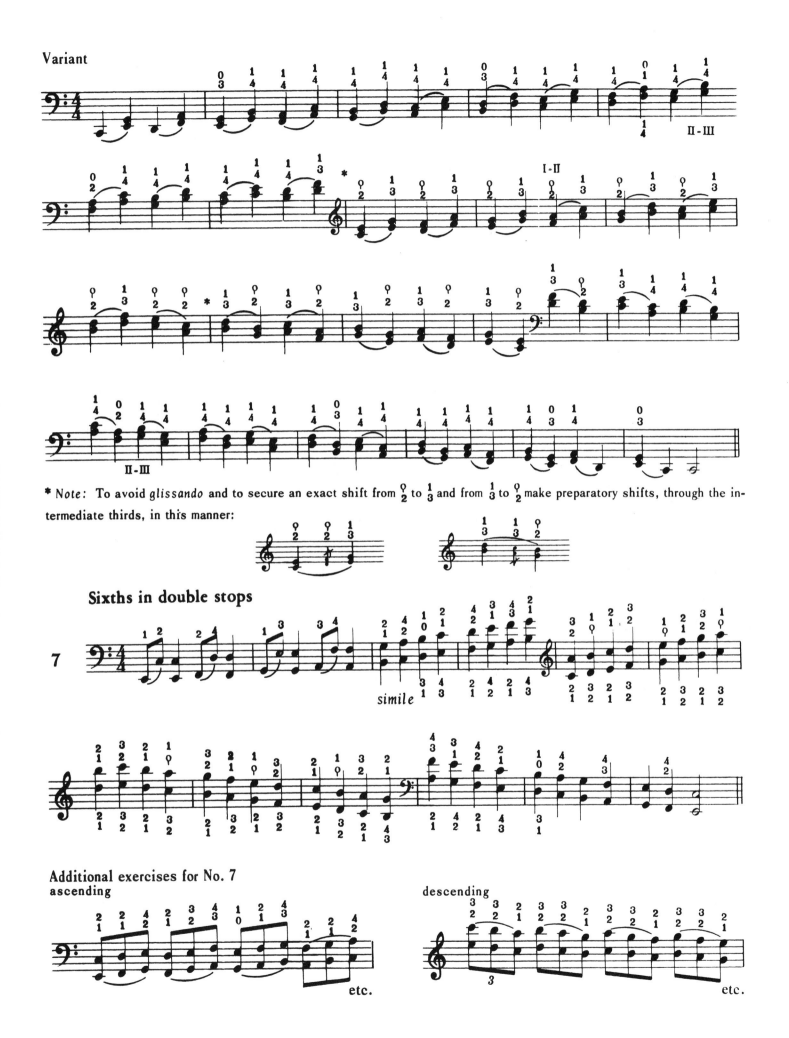

* *Note*: To avoid *glissando* and to secure an exact shift from $\frac{0}{2}$ to $\frac{1}{3}$ and from $\frac{1}{3}$ to $\frac{0}{2}$ make preparatory shifts, through the intermediate thirds, in this manner:

Sixths in double stops

7

Additional exercises for No. 7

ascending

descending

etc.

etc.

Variant

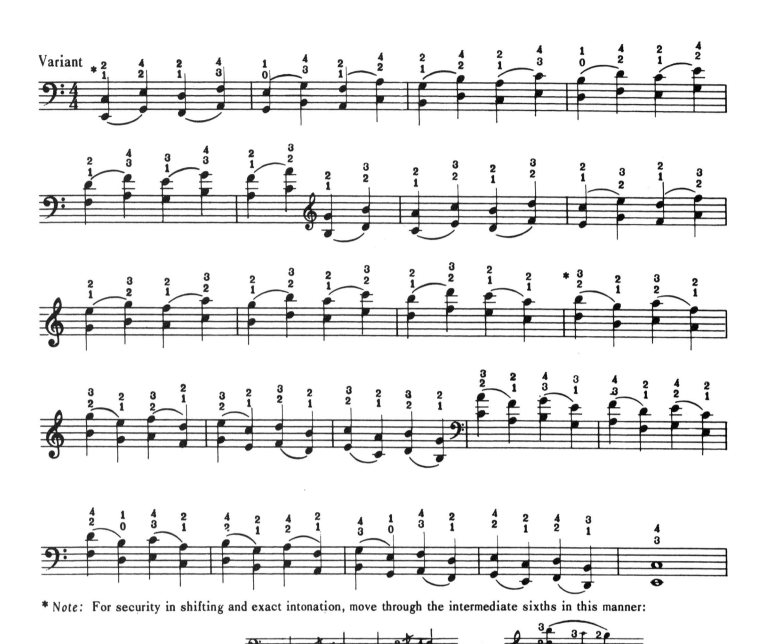

* Note: For security in shifting and exact intonation, move through the intermediate sixths in this manner:

Octaves

8

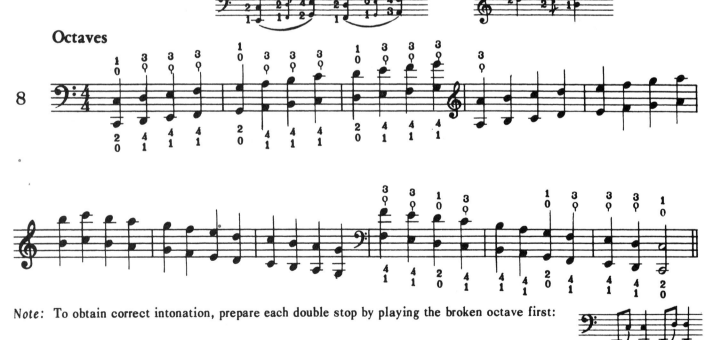

Note: To obtain correct intonation, prepare each double stop by playing the broken octave first:

etc.

Arpeggio in double stops

Scale in chords

Chromatic scale

Scale in natural and artificial harmonics

Note: The "natural" harmonics are represented by round white notes and are produced by placing the finger lightly on the *indicated string* at the point shown; the "artificial" harmonics are represented by diamond-shaped notes and are sounded by placing the finger lightly on the string above the *firmly-pressed* tones (shown in black) played by first finger or thumb as called for.

Actual pitches (3-8ve Scale)

Produced in this manner:

(Same fingerings descending)

A MINOR

Triad with inversions (short arpeggios)

Variant

Thirds in double stops

Sixths

Note: For complete mastery of No. 8, these sixths should also be practiced as double stops:
etc.

14

G MAJOR

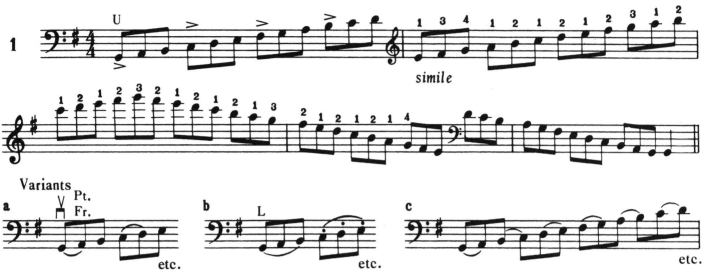

1

Variants

a   Pt. Fr. etc.

b   L   etc.

c   etc.

Note: Nos. 1, 2, and 3 should be played with a firm bow and secure grip (*forte*).

Thirds

2

Arpeggios

a Tonic

3

The lower fingering to be played entirely on G-string.

b Sub-dominant

Use same fingerings on all strings.

Dominant seventh

4

Triad with inversions (short arpeggios)

5

Note: It is suggested that two bowing styles be used. 1) Lower half, with the shortened notes played "flying staccato" 2) Upper half, with a sharp martellato for staccato notes.

Variant

Note: Play these with short strokes in lower half, middle, and upper half of bow.

Thirds in double stops

6

Variants

a   b   c

Sixths in double stops

7

Note: Use same bowing variants as with thirds, in No. 6.

16

Octaves

Broken thirds and octaves

Octave arpeggios

a Tonic

b Sub-dominant

Arpeggio in double stops

Additional exercise:

etc.

Scale in chords

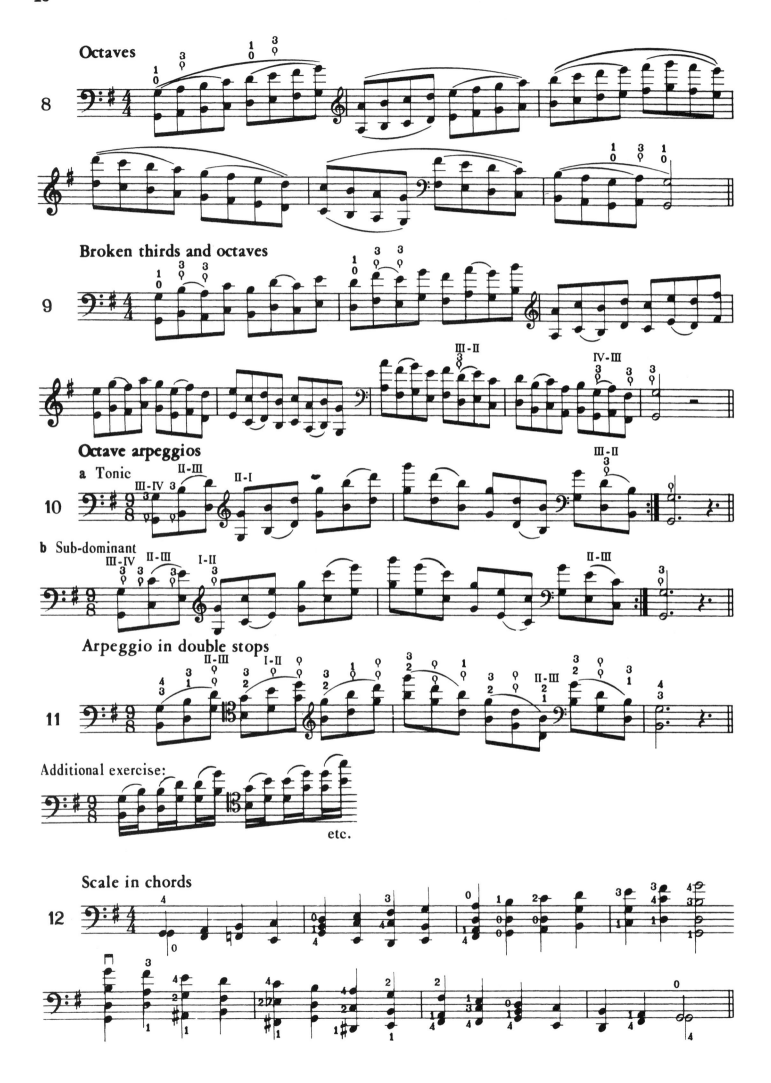

E MINOR

1

Note: In a moderate tempo these exercises (1-6) should be played *spiccato,* the bow to be held lightly by thumb, index and little finger; at a faster tempo a short *detaché (sautillé),* weighted with thumb, index and 3rd finger should be used.

Thirds

Arpeggios

a Tonic

b Sub-dominant

Diminished seventh

Augmented triad

Triad with inversions (short arpeggios)

Variants

Variant

For supplementary exercises, see **a** and **b** above.

*For supplementary exercises, see C - major section, No. 12, (p. 7).

F MAJOR

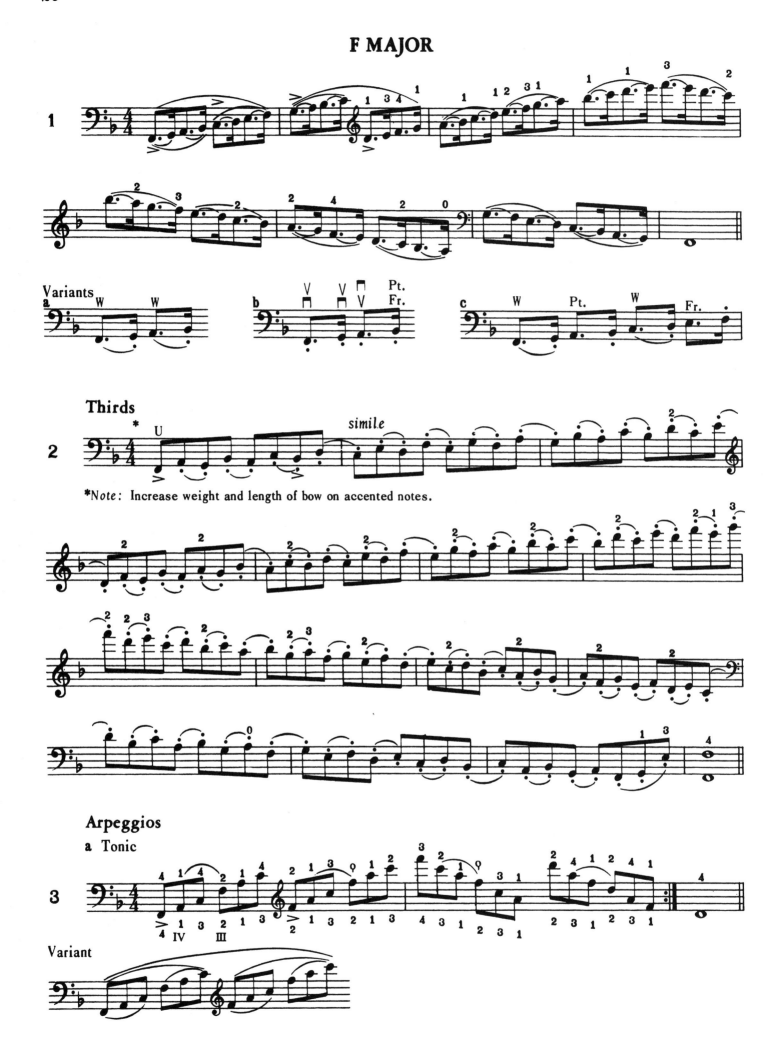

*Note: Increase weight and length of bow on accented notes.

b Sub-dominant

Dominant seventh — simile

4

Variant — Pt.

Triad with inversions (short arpeggios)

5 — Fr.

Variant

22

D MINOR

24

Augmented triad

Triad with inversions (short arpeggios)

Variant

Thirds (double-stop fingerings)

Sixths

Octaves

Chromatic scale in octaves

D MAJOR

Variants

Note: Pay special attention to rhythmic accuracy and to smoothness in transition from ♩♩ to ♩♩♩ to ♩♩♩

Thirds

Arpeggios

a Tonic

b Sub-dominant

Dominant seventh

Triad with inversions (short arpeggios)

Variant

Thirds (double-stop fingerings)

28

Sixths

7

Octaves

8

Variant

etc.

Broken thirds and octaves

9

Octave arpeggios

a Tonic

b Sub-dominant

Dominant seventh

Octave scale (alternating fingerings)

Tenths

Arpeggio in double stops

Scale in chords

B MINOR

Diminished seventh

Augmented triad

Triad with inversions (short arpeggios)

Variant

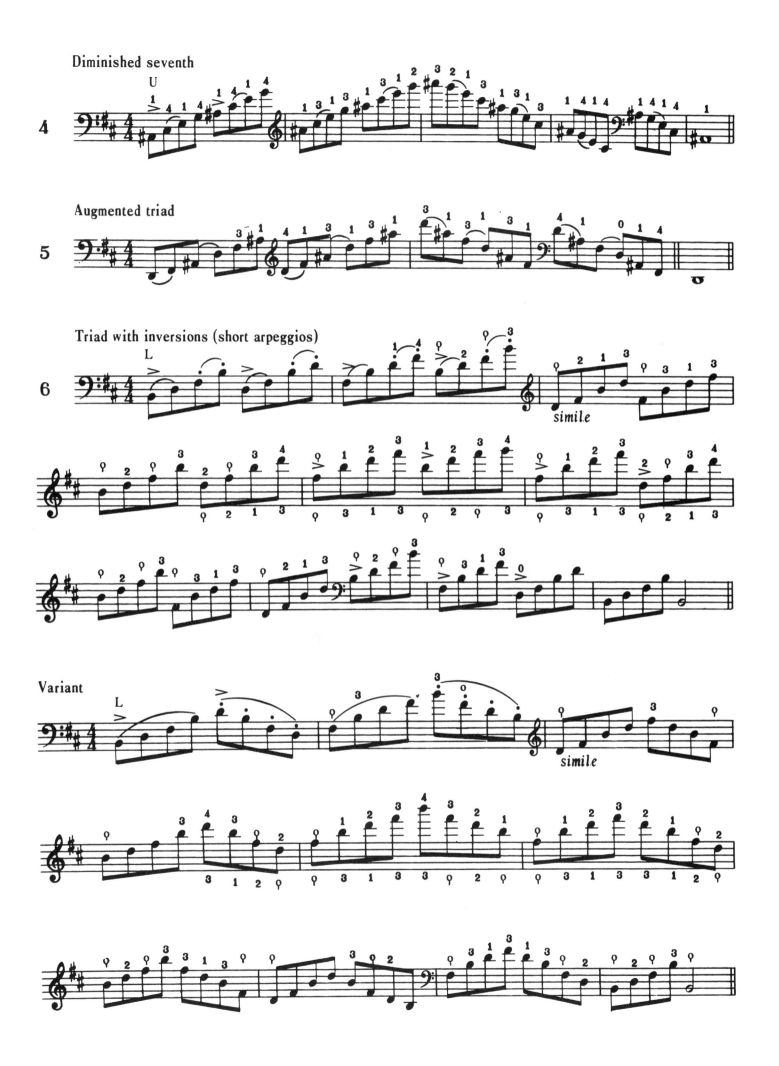

32

Thirds in double stops

Additional exercise

Play easily, without excessive wrist and arm movements.

etc.

Sixths in double stops

Additional exercise

Play easily, without excessive wrist and arm movements.

etc.

Octaves

Variant

etc.

Broken thirds and octaves

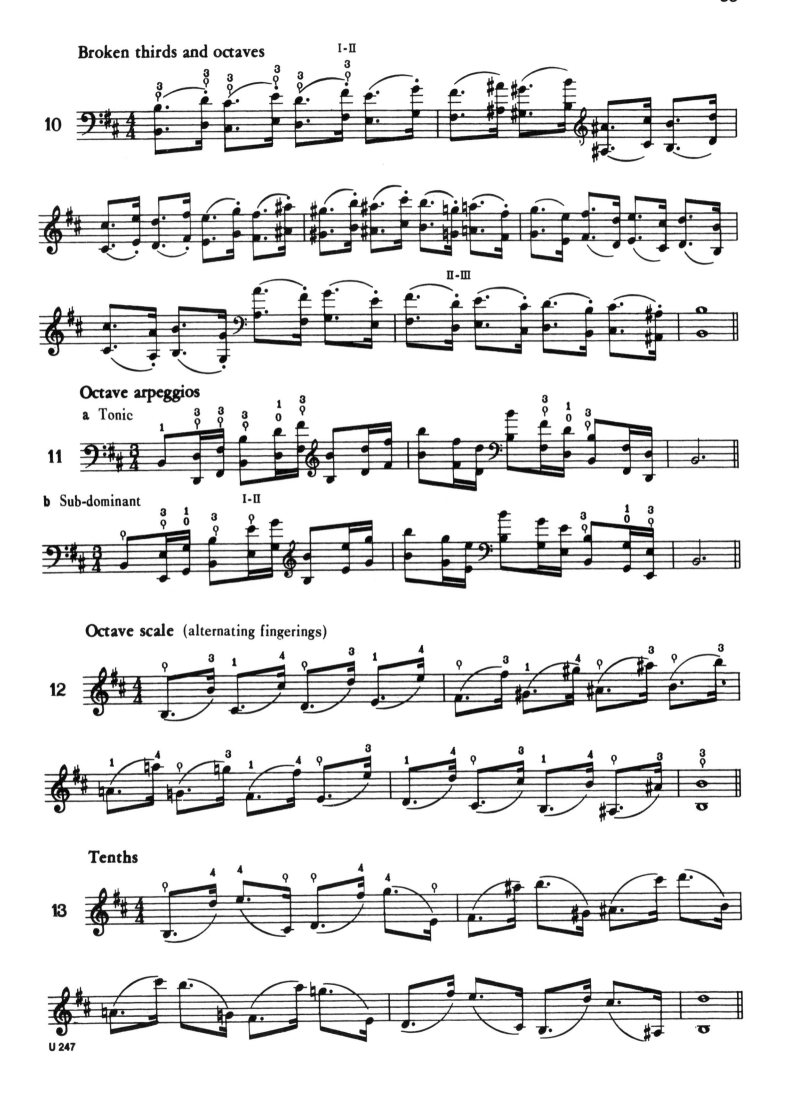

Octave arpeggios

a Tonic

b Sub-dominant

Octave scale (alternating fingerings)

Tenths

B-FLAT MAJOR

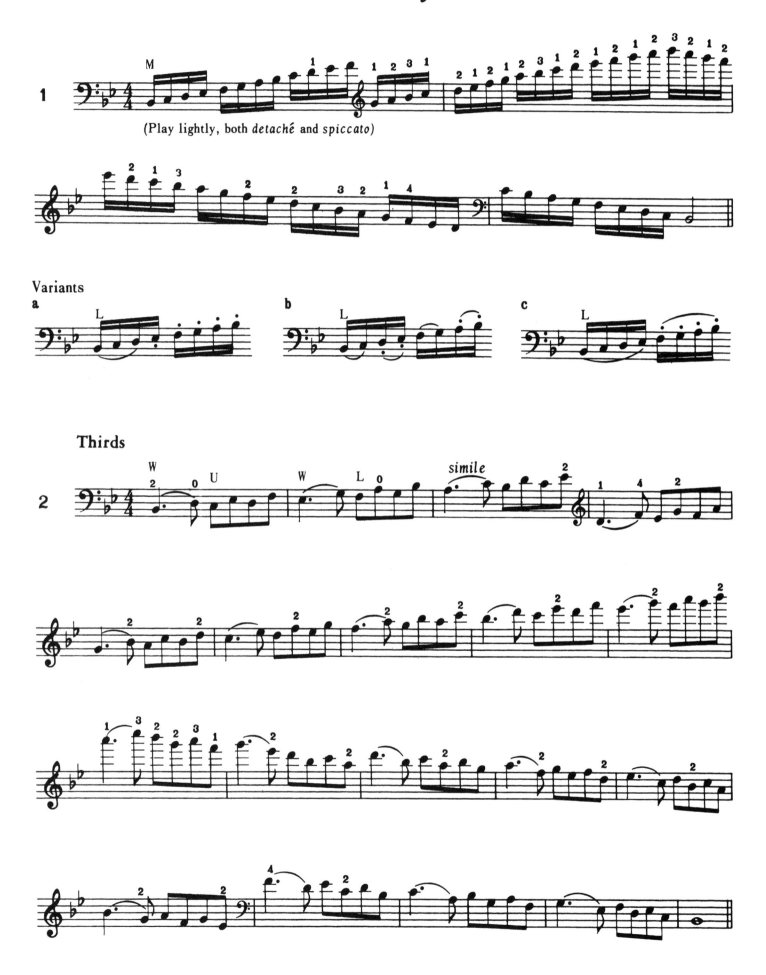

1 (Play lightly, both *detaché* and *spiccato*)

Variants

a **b** **c**

Thirds

2 *simile*

Arpeggios

a Tonic

b Sub-dominant

Dominant seventh

Triad with inversions (short arpeggios)

staccato

Variant

simile

Thirds (double-stop fingerings)

(Play lightly, both *detaché* and *staccato*)

Sixths

Octaves

spiccato   *simile*

Broken thirds and octaves

Octave arpeggios
a Tonic

b Sub-dominant

Arpeggio in double stops

Supplementary exercise :

etc.

Scale in chords

G MINOR

Variant

Thirds

Variants

Arpeggios
a Tonic

b Sub-dominant

*Note: When moving from ♪ to ♩. it is recommended that the longer notes be attacked with an increase of bow speed. In this way the essential stress on the first and third beats of each measure is achieved.

Sixths in double stops

Broken thirds and octaves

Octave arpeggios
a Tonic
b Sub-dominant

* At the beginning of this exercise the thumb should stop the D-string at E♭.

A MAJOR

Triad with inversions (short arpeggios)

Variants

Variant

Thirds in double stops

Sixths in double stops

* Note: Play with the lower half of the bow, using "flying staccato;" or the upper half, using *martellato*.

F-SHARP MINOR

Thirds (double-stop fingerings)

E-FLAT MAJOR

Triad with inversions (short arpeggios)

5

Variant

Thirds in double stops

6

C MINOR

Variants

Thirds

Arpeggios
a Tonic

b Sub-dominant

Diminished seventh

Augmented triad

Triad with inversions (short arpeggios)

staccato

simile

Variant

simile

Thirds in double stops

*This sequence may be omitted if desired.

Sixths in double stops

Octaves

Octave scale (alternating fingerings)

Tenths

E MAJOR

Thirds

Arpeggios
a Tonic

b Sub-dominant

Dominant seventh

Triad with inversions (short arpeggios)

Variant

Variant

Thirds (double-stop fingerings)

Variants
a   b

Sixths

Variants

Octaves

C-SHARP MINOR

58

Augmented triad

5

Triad with inversions (short arpeggios)

6

staccato

simile

Variant

"flying staccato"

Variant

simile

Thirds in double stops

7

Sixths in double stops

8

Octaves

Broken thirds and octaves

Octave arpeggios
a Tonic

b Sub-dominant

A-FLAT MAJOR

1

2 Thirds

* When using lower fingering prepare the thumb on Bb as the 3rd finger reaches the preceding Eb.

3 Arpeggios
a Tonic

b Sub-dominant

4 Dominant seventh

62

F MINOR

64

Sixths

8

Octaves

9

Broken thirds and octaves

10

Octave arpeggios

a Tonic

11

b Sub-dominant

66

B MAJOR

68

G-SHARP MINOR

*Note: Nos. 1-6 to be played lightly both *detaché* and *staccato*.

Variant

Thirds

Variant

Arpeggios
a Tonic

b Sub-dominant

Diminished seventh

Augmented triad

Triad with inversions (short arpeggios)

Variant

etc.

Variant

Thirds (double-stop fingerings)

7

Sixths in double stops

8

Octaves

9

D-FLAT MAJOR

Triad with inversions (short arpeggios)

Variant

Thirds in double stops

Sixths in double stops

Octaves

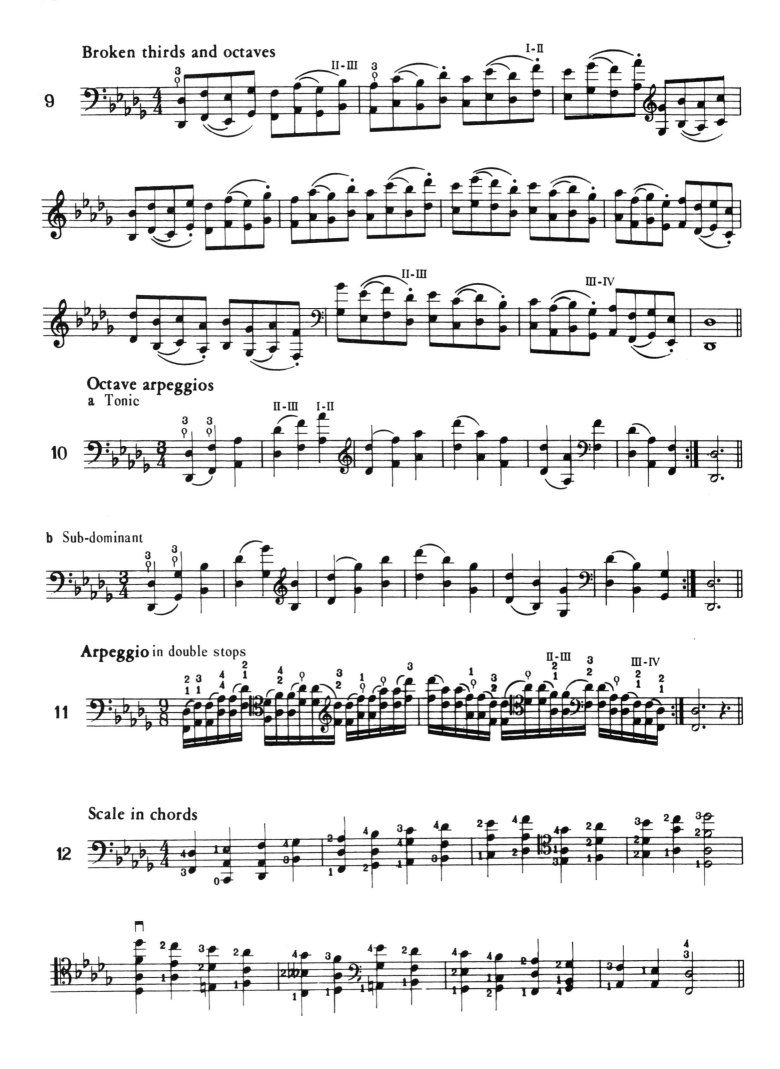

B-FLAT MINOR

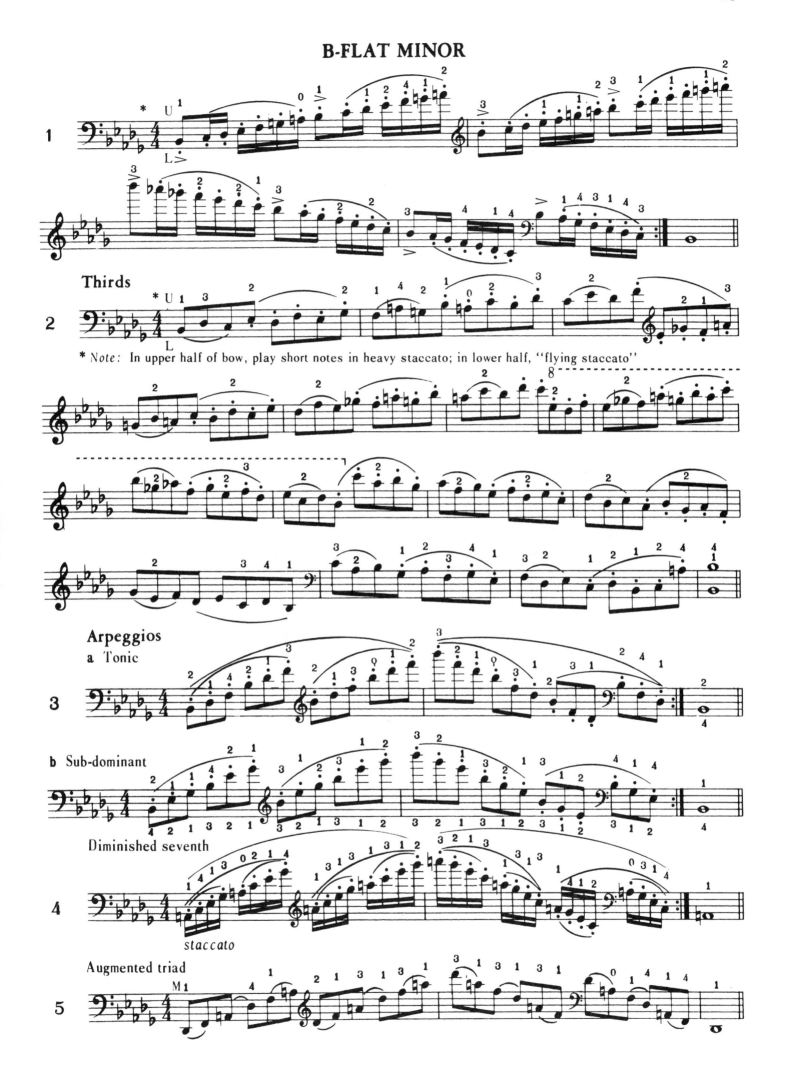

Thirds

* *Note:* In upper half of bow, play short notes in heavy staccato; in lower half, "flying staccato"

Arpeggios
a Tonic

b Sub-dominant

Diminished seventh

staccato

Augmented triad

Triad with inversions (short arpeggios)

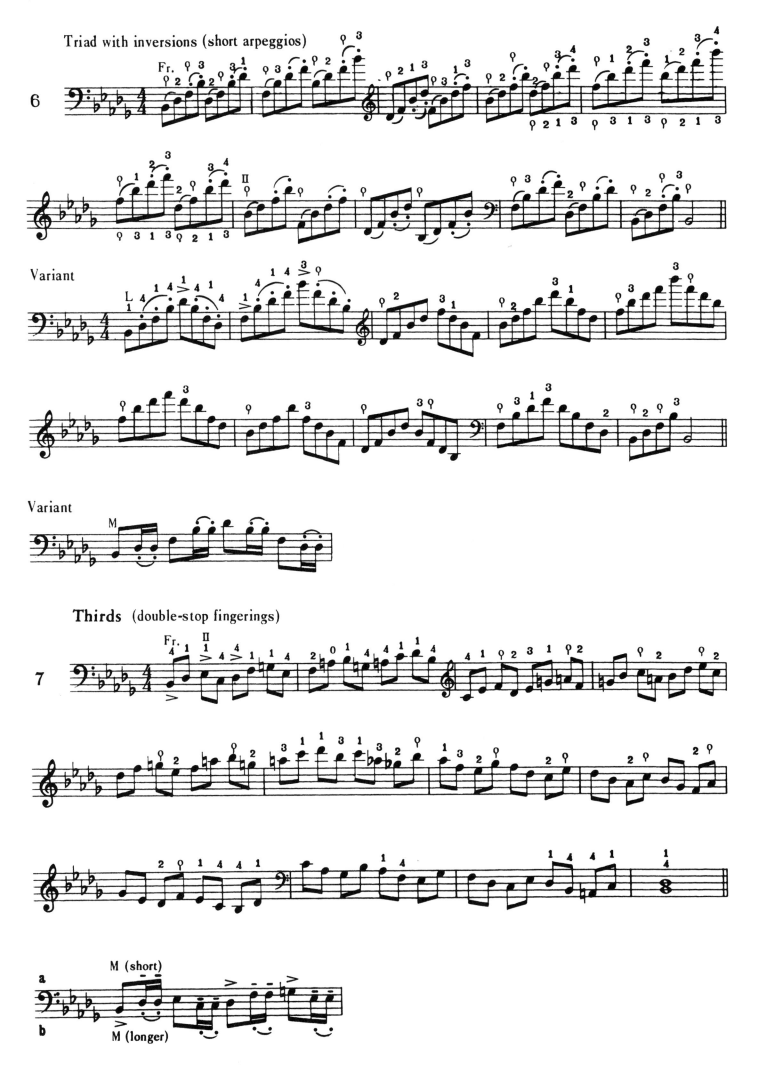

Variant

Variant

Thirds (double-stop fingerings)

Sixths

8

Octaves

9

Broken thirds and octaves

10

Arpeggios
a Tonic

11

b Sub-dominant

F-SHARP MAJOR

Triad with inversions (short arpeggios)

5

Variant

Thirds (double-stop fingerings)

6

80

Sixths

7

Octaves

8

Arpeggio in double stops

9

Scale in chords

10

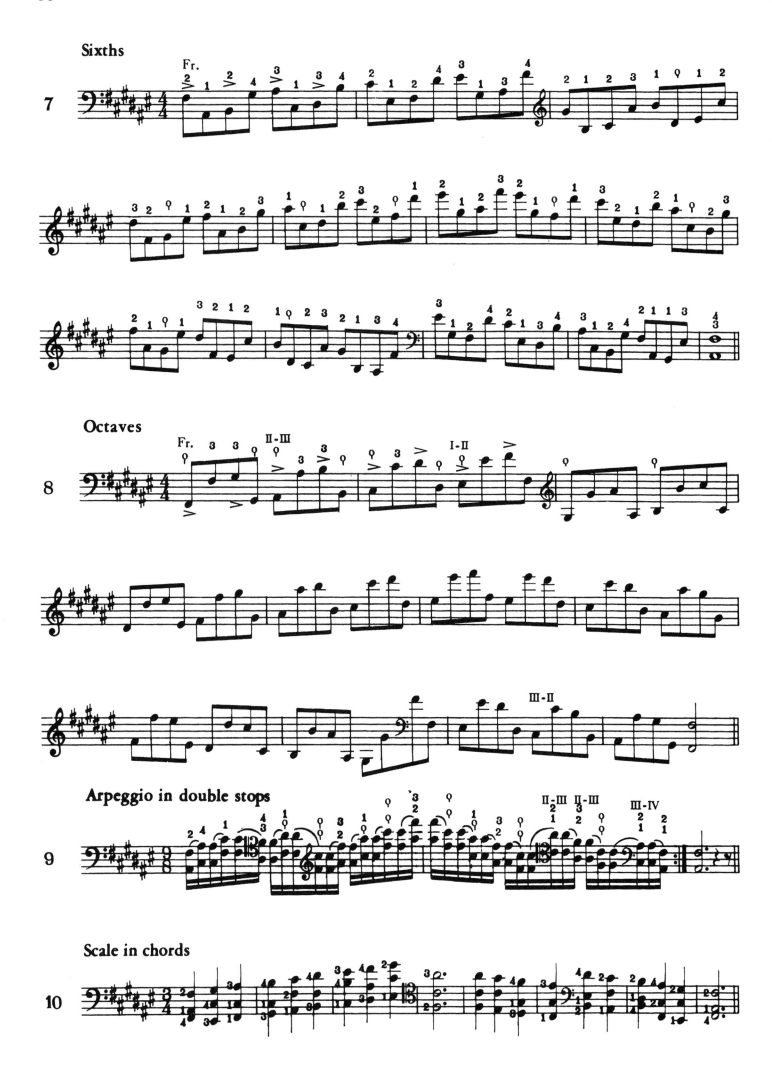

E-FLAT MINOR

Thirds

Arpeggios

a Tonic

b Sub-dominant

Diminished seventh

Augmented triad

Triad with inversions (short arpeggios)

Variant

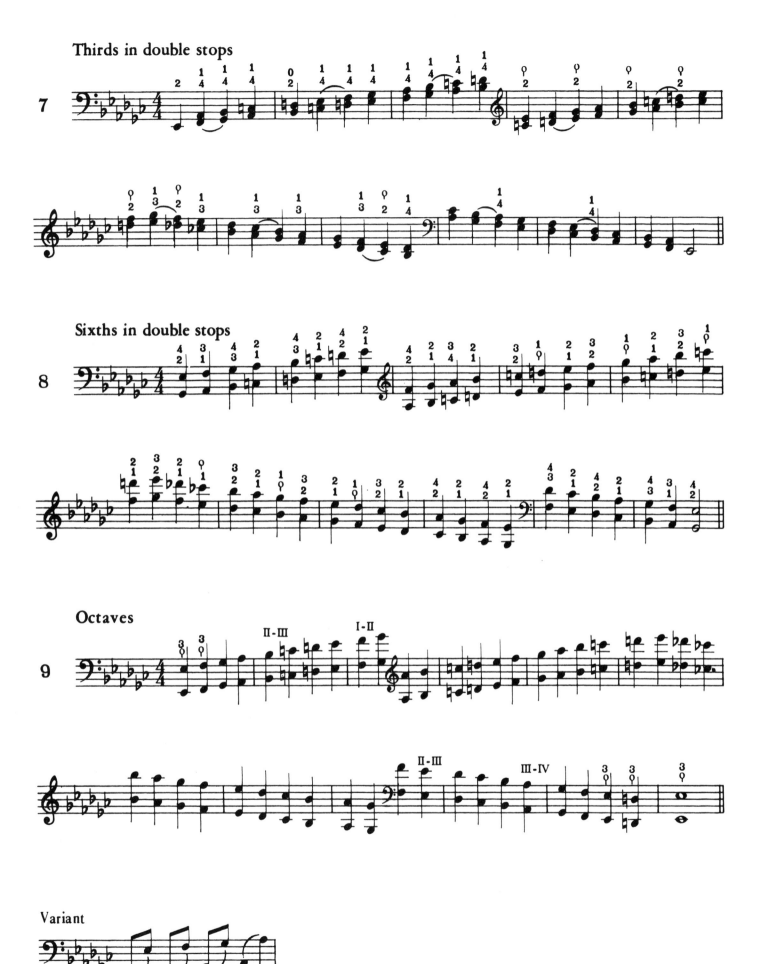

Thirds in double stops

Sixths in double stops

Octaves

Variant

etc.